D0583565

Animals on the Farm
Horses

Aaron Carr

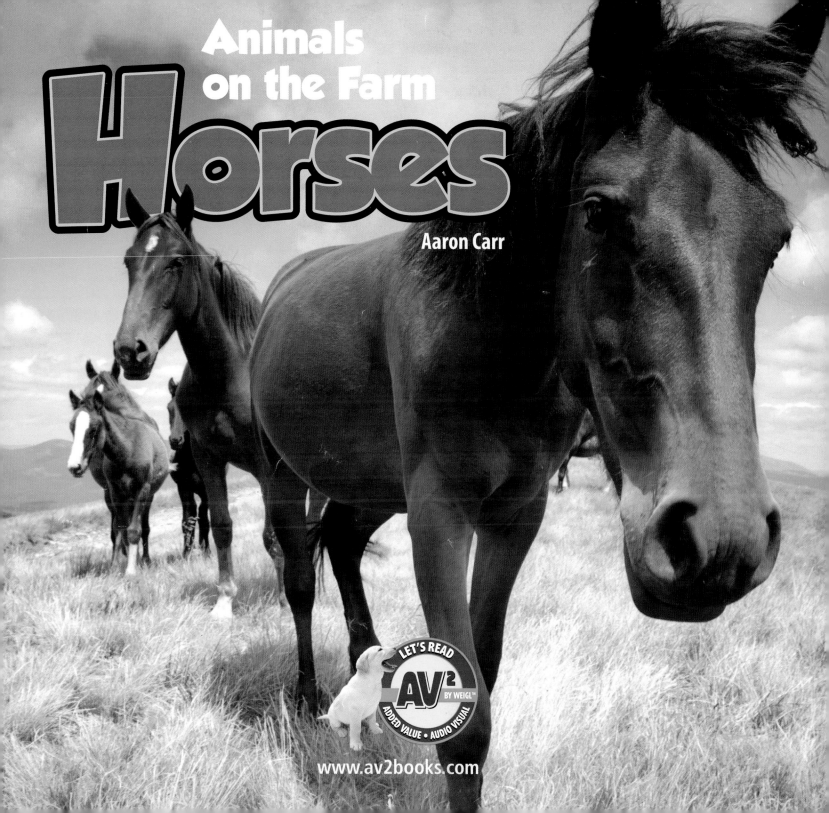

www.av2books.com

Go to **www.av2books.com**, and enter this book's unique code.

BOOK CODE

Y357635

AV² by Weigl brings you media enhanced books that support active learning.

AV² provides enriched content that supplements and complements this book. Weigl's AV² books strive to create inspired learning and engage young minds in a total learning experience.

Your AV² Media Enhanced books come alive with...

Audio
Listen to sections of the book read aloud.

Video
Watch informative video clips.

Embedded Weblinks
Gain additional information for research.

Try This!
Complete activities and hands-on experiments.

Key Words
Study vocabulary, and complete a matching word activity.

Quizzes
Test your knowledge.

Slide Show
View images and captions, and prepare a presentation.

...and much, much more!

Published by AV² by Weigl
350 5th Avenue, 59th Floor   New York, NY 10118
Website: www.av2books.com   www.weigl.com

Library of Congress Cataloging-in-Publication Data
Carr, Aaron.
Horses / Aaron Carr.
     pages cm. -- (Animals on the farm)
ISBN 978-1-62127-232-8 (hardcover : alkaline paper) -- ISBN 978-1-62127-236-6 (softcover : alkaline paper)
1. Horses--Juvenile literature. 2. Farm animals--Juvenile literature. I. Title.
SF302.C34 2013
636.1--dc23

                           2012044716

Printed in the United States of America in North Mankato, Minnesota
1 2 3 4 5 6 7 8 9 0   17 16 15 14 13

022013
WEP300113

Senior Editor: Aaron Carr   Art Director: Terry Paulhus

Weigl acknowledges Getty Images as the primary image supplier for this title.

Animals on the Farm
Horses

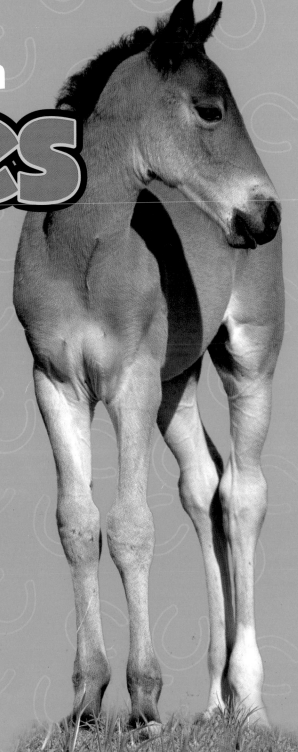

CONTENTS

I am a big farm animal. Farmers keep me to do work around the farm.

I am a mammal. My large body is covered with short fur.
I have long hair down my neck and on my tail.

I have four long legs.
My legs help me run and work.

I have very good eyesight.
I have bigger eyes
than any other mammal
that lives on land.

11

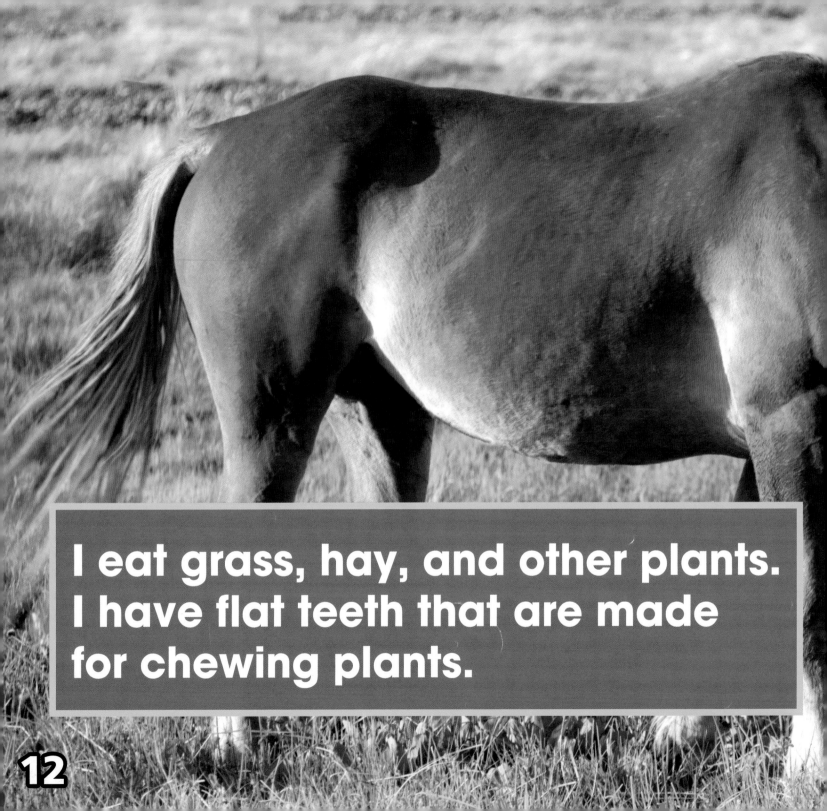

I eat grass, hay, and other plants. I have flat teeth that are made for chewing plants.

How do I talk to other animals?
I "neigh" to let them know
I am there.

I am very friendly. I like to live with many other horses.

I give birth to my baby in the spring.

My baby is called a foal.

Foals can walk right after birth. They are full grown after three years.

21

HORSE FACTS

These pages provide detailed information that expands on the interesting facts found in the book. These pages are intended to be used by adults to help young readers round out their knowledge of each amazing animal featured in the *Animals on the Farm* series.

Pages 4-5

Farmers keep horses for riding and doing work. The horse was domesticated about 6,000 years ago. Since then, people have used horses on farms, to carry people from place to place, and even for recreational riding. On ranches, horses are still used to help ranchers manage large herds of cows or other livestock.

Pages 6–7

Horses are mammals. They belong to the equine family, which includes zebras and donkeys. There is only one species of horse, though there are different types, called breeds. Horse breeds can be divided into three groups. Draft horses are large workhorses, light horses are smaller and used for riding, and ponies are the smallest.

Pages 8–9

Horses have four long legs. Horses can run at speeds greater than 40 miles (65 kilometers) per hour. Draft horses may stand 80 inches (200 centimeters) tall at the withers, or the highest part of the shoulder. A horse that stands about 58 inches (147 cm) or lower is considered a pony.

Pages 10–11

Horses have very good eyesight. Horses have the largest eyes of any land mammal. Their high-set eyes give them a much wider field of vision than humans. Horses have blind spots, including directly in front of the nose, under the chin, and directly behind the head.

Horses eat grass and other plants. Horses are herbivores, or plant-eaters. In nature, horses graze on many types of grass. Horses kept on farms and ranches are usually fed a mixture of hay and horse feed. The feed is a mixture of grains, oats, vegetables, and minerals.

Horses talk to other animals by neighing. They also make a sound called a whinny. Horses can use their ears to communicate. Ears flat back against the head mean a horse is angry. Pricked up ears mean the horse is alert.

Horses like to live with many other horses. Horses are social animals. They prefer to be in groups, called herds. In nature, a single male horse, called a stallion, will lead the herd. When two horses meet, they will greet each other by sniffing at each other's noses.

 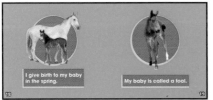

Horses give birth to their babies in the spring. Horses give birth after 11 months of pregnancy. Newborn horses are called foals. They can weigh 100 pounds (45 kilograms) at birth. Foals will drink their mother's milk for the first six months of their life.

Baby horses can walk when they are born. Foals grow quickly. Between six months and four years of age, male horses are called colts and females are called fillies. Horses are fully grown by five years of age. They can live for 20 to 30 years.

KEY WORDS

Research has shown that as much as 65 percent of all written material published in English is made up of 300 words. These 300 words cannot be taught using pictures or learned by sounding them out. They must be recognized by sight. This book contains 55 common sight words to help young readers improve their reading fluency and comprehension. This book also teaches young readers several important content words. These words are paired with pictures to aid in learning and improve understanding.

Page	Sight Words First Appearance
5	a, am, animal, around, big, do, farm, I, keep, me, the, to, work
6	and, down, have, is, large, long, my, on, with
8	four, help, run
10	any, eyes, good, land, lives, other, than, that, very
12	are, eat, for, made, plants
15	how, know, let, talk, them, there
16	like, many
18	give, in
20	after, can, right, they, three, years

Page	Content Words First Appearance
5	farmers
6	body, fur, hair, mammal, neck, tail
8	legs
10	eyesight
12	grass, hay, teeth
16	horses
18	baby, spring
19	foal